To order additional copies of *The FACTory*, by Michael Warren,
call 1-800-765-6955.

Visit us at www.reviewandherald.com for information on other
Review and Herald products.

Guide PRESENTS . . .

The **FACTORY**

A TINY **HUGE COLLECTION OF COOL AND CRAZY FACTS**

Compiled by
Michael Warren

REVIEW AND HERALD® PUBLISHING ASSOCIATION
HAGERSTOWN, MD 21740

The author assumes full responsibility for the accuracy of all facts and quotations as cited in this book.

Unless otherwise noted, all Scripture quotations are from the *Holy Bible, New International Version.* Copyright © 1973, 1978, 1985, International Bible Society. Used by permission of Zondervan Bible Publishers.

Edited by Randy Fishell
Interior art by Randy Verougstraete
Cover designed by Madelyn Ruiz
Interior designed by Tina M. Ivany
Electronic page makeup by Tina M. Ivany
Cover art by Ron Wheeler
Typeset: 11/14 Veljovic Medium

PRINTED IN U.S.A.

05   04   03   02   01   5   4   3   2   1

R&H Cataloging Service
Warren, Michael, comp.
    The factory: a tiny huge collection of cool and crazy facts.

    1. Curiosities and wonders.   2. Nature-miscellanea.   I. Guide.

                                030

ISBN 0-8280-1556-2

CONTENTS

CREATURES GREAT AND SMALL
FACTS ABOUT ANIMALS, INSECTS, AND REPTILES

A COAL A DAY
Monkeys on the island of Zanzibar have a most unusual eating habit—they like to munch on charcoal. Charcoal has the ability to absorb toxins, which allows the monkeys to eat leaves that would otherwise be poisonous. —*Discover*

LIZARD LANGUAGE
Have you ever wondered why lizards do "push-ups"? It's to communicate with other lizards. Depending on the circumstances, a lizard doing push-ups might be attracting a mate, warning away competitors, or establishing territory. —*Outside*

SNAKE'S PARADISE

In some parts of Guam there are 12,000 snakes per square mile— the highest concentration of snakes anywhere in the world.

—*Outside*

LANDSCAPING BY BUCKY BEAVER

While most plants and animals adapt to the environment in which they live, beavers do just the opposite. They change the environment to suit their own needs. They build lakes and dams to protect their lodges, which have underwater entrances.

—*Audubon*

OUCH—I DID IT AGAIN!

Porcupine quills are coated with an antibiotic that fights infection. This is helpful to the prickly critters because they sometimes stab themselves with their own sharp quills. —*Omni*

BEE AN UNDERTAKER

In the complex society of a beehive, every bee has a job to do. Some bees even serve as "undertakers" to remove dead bees from the hive. But apparently it's not a favorite job. Undertaker bees spend only about a day in that "career" before moving on to other work. New workers must constantly replace them. —*Science News*

SUPER EARS

The long-eared bat, found in Europe and Africa, has hearing so good that it can detect a moth in flight. —*Ripley's Believe It or Not!*

TRACK STAR BUGS

Some tiger beetles can run at a speed of two feet per second. To cover the same distance in relation to its size, a racehorse would have to run 250 miles per hour. —*National Geographic*

GARFIELD, YOU SHOULDN'T HAVE

Cats can be lovable, but they often have no respect for their feathered friends. In the state of Wisconsin alone, kitties kill about 19 million songbirds each year. One way to protect the birds in your backyard is to put a bell on your cat's collar, which may warn birds of approaching danger. —*Falcon*

BORING INSECT

One kind of woodboring beetle can live more than 50 years. —*Ranger Rick*

CHILL OUT

A tiny insect called a midge doesn't mind cold a bit. In fact, some midge larvae have survived after a bath in liquid helium—which is 454 degrees below zero! —*Ranger Rick*

MOSQUITO TARGETS

Why do some people seem to attract mosquitoes more than other people do? Mosquitoes notice color contrast, movement, and the temperature and humidity of your skin. But most of all, they're attracted by smell. Every time you breathe out and exhale carbon dioxide you're alerting mosquitoes to your presence—up to 50 feet away. Your skin also gives off other chemicals, such as lactic acid, octenol, and even the smell from odor-producing bacteria in the feet. —*Discover*

DEADLY DATING

Male fireflies have to be especially careful whom they choose for a mate. That's because the female of one species likes to imitate the blinking pattern of her rival from another species so she can eat the male. If an unhappy male firefly makes a bad choice, he'll end up as lunch! —*Discover*

SWEET DEDICATION

The average worker bee makes just $1/12$ teaspoon of honey in its entire lifetime. A single pound of honey requires about 640,000 miles' worth of flights by worker bees. —*React* and *Whad'ya Knowledge*

LIZARD SUNSCREEN

As you may have noticed, lizards can hang out on sunny rocks all day long without getting burned. So how do they do it? They have their own kind of sunscreen—a thick layer of dead skin cells that protects them.

—*Reader's Digest*

DOWN IN THE MOUTH

The darkling beetle lives in the driest of African deserts, and it has a unique way to find water. Every morning as dew forms on its shiny shell, the beetle tilts forward so the water drops down into its mouth.
—*National Geographic*

STRETCHY AND STRONG

The silk produced by the golden orb spider is stronger than steel and more elastic than rubber. —*Newsweek*

CHEW ON THIS

When exposed to hard rock music, termites chewed through wood two times faster than normal. —*USA Today*

MAN! I'M HUNGRY!

TOOTHY LIZARDS

The name *alligator* comes from the Spanish word *el lagarto*, which means "the lizard." —*Wildlife Fact File*

THROUGH THICK AND THIN

Most people have about 100,000 hairs on their head. Dogs, however, have up to 60,000 hairs *per square inch*. Sea otters sport up to 1 *million* hairs per square inch. —*National Geographic*

NATURAL MEDICINE

Animals sometimes use plants as medicines. Some chimpanzees eat bitter-tasting aspilia plants to kill harmful parasites. Kodiak bears chew up a certain root and rub it on their fur to kill fungus.

—*National Geographic World*

HELP YOURSELF, JO JO

When a car hit Jo Jo, a Labrador retriever in Kentucky, he limped off to get help. In spite of his bruises, the dog walked about a mile to the animal hospital and "checked" himself in. Jo Jo had often stayed at the animal hospital when his master was away, so he knew right where to go. —*Parade*

COLLECT 'EM ALL

The Florida Everglades is home to 67 different species of mosquitoes.
—*Outside*

STEALTH EATER

One brown bat can catch 600 mosquitoes in an hour. —*Boys' Life*

YUM, Y'ALL.

POWER SNIFFERS

Polar bears hunt by sense of smell, and they can detect a dead whale from 20 miles away. —*Wildlife Fact File*

KINDA CREEPY

There are about 40,000 different kinds of spiders in the world, most of which are harmless. In the United States, the two most dangerous spiders are the black widow and the brown recluse.
—*UC Berkeley Wellness Letter*

TERMITE MANSIONS

In the tropics termites sometimes build elaborate nests made from soil that they plaster together with their saliva. They build these mounds as high as 20 feet, with basements 15 feet deep!
—*Outside*

> JUST MY LUCK! I LIVE ON THE TOP FLOOR!

NO MAPS NEEDED

When a bee finds a new source of honey, it tells the other bees where it is located by doing one of 2,000 different "waggle dances."
—*Ripley's Believe It or Not!*

HOP TO IT

Powerful leg muscles enable fleas to jump distances up to 200 times their body length. —Ocala *Star-Banner*

CHANCE OF LEECHES

When it rains in some parts of Australia, certain sneaky leeches climb trees and wait for animals to pass underneath. When they drop on their prey, the leech feels just like a raindrop. That way the animal doesn't even know the leech is attached until it's too late!

—*Ranger Rick*

MISSING FIREFLIES

"Lightning bugs" are disappearing fast. They used to be plentiful during summer months, but these days they're getting harder and harder to find. The biggest problem is loss of habitat. However, the Japanese are so fond of fireflies that they have set up sanctuaries to protect them.

—*Wall Street Journal*

WORLD'S SMALLEST "PORCUPINE"

A tiny millipede has barbs that work in similar fashion to those of a porcupine. When attacked by an ant, the millipede lets loose its quills. As the ant struggles to free itself from the barbs, their sharp points only dig deeper, eventually killing the ant.

—*Popular Science*

LIZARD COLONISTS

New Zealand's endangered tuatara lizards can grow up to two feet long, but they're fast disappearing. Scientists there came up with a new way to help the lizards. They started a new colony on an island on which the lizards used to live. —*Science News*

FLIES ON THE RISE

Two household flies can produce 190 *septillion* baby flies in just five months. That's 190 followed by 24 zeroes. Fortunately, not all these babies survive to maturity.

—*Junior Guide*

TIME FOR YOUR CHECK-UP

Around 145,000 cats and 281,000 dogs visit the veterinarian each day. —*On an Average Day . . .*

PASS THE SWEATER, PLEASE

Moth caterpillars love to munch on wool sweaters that are left for long periods of time in a dark place (such as your closet). But moths don't bother sheep. That's because sheep move around too much and live in the cold and rain. —*Ranger Rick*

NON-STOP CHOPPERS

Alligators grow a new set of teeth as each old set wears down. In a lifetime a 'gator can go through up to 3,000 teeth! —*React*

SNAKES ALIVE!

Famous archaeologist Howard Carter (who found the tomb of King Tut) had to stop work on one of his digs in Egypt after only two weeks. The reason? Too many cobras!

—*Horn Archaeological Museum Newsletter*

20

LAB AND TECH TREK
FACTS ABOUT SCIENCE, GEOLOGY, AND TECHNOLOGY

COMPUTER SMALL TALK
Years ago few people imagined how small and powerful computers would be. In 1949 *Popular Mechanics* magazine made this prediction: "Computers in the future may weigh no more than 1.5 tons."

—*Intel Corporation*

BOUNCE ME AN EGG
Eggs in northern Alaska, where the temperature can reach 60 degrees below zero, can be bounced like rubber balls if they are left outside for a long time. —*Ripley's Believe It or Not!*

EXPLODING WHEAT

When grain is stored in "elevators" (big storage containers), it can become explosive. When very dry dust from the wheat or other grain is stored under pressure, just one spark can set it off. That's why many grain elevators now have safety devices to prevent explosions. —New York *Times*

LAKE IN THE OCEAN

Scientists have discovered a lake *the size of Lake Ontario* in Antarctica. The lake is 5,000 square miles in size and 1,600 feet deep. The lake is buried under more than two miles of ice, which keeps it insulated from the extreme cold on the surface. —*Discover*

ZINC SANDWICH

All pennies made since 1982 are made of zinc. The only copper in them is a thin layer on the outside. —*Zillions*

MUSIC TO MAKE YOU SMARTER

British scientists have discovered that listening to Mozart boosts your IQ, but for only about 15 minutes. They think the complex music may stimulate your brain's activity. —*Newsweek*

DOES THE NFL KNOW ABOUT THIS?

When you toss a coin into the air, it's more likely to land "tails up." That's because the head side weighs more. —*USA Today*

THEORY OF POTATO RELATIVITY

Tell Mom you've got a formula for perfectly cooking a potato of any size. It's $T = r^2/c$. T is the cooking time, r is the radius of the potato, and c is the constant that depends on the water's heat capacity and the diffusivity of the water and the potato. Huh? —*Omni*

DON'T BE A DRIP

A leaky faucet can waste a lot of water. *One drop per second* will add up to *6,000 gallons* of wasted water each year. — *Youth!*

MONEY TO BURN

Every year the government throws away 7,000 tons of worn-out money—about $79.6 billion worth. Some banks are now recycling old bills by turning them into roof shingles, stationery, and even fuel. — *Outside Kids*

ROUND RAINBOWS

One reason you can't find an end of a rainbow is that they're round. The part you're seeing is the portion that is above the horizon. You can sometimes see round rainbows below you when flying in an airplane. — *Romance Emporium*

GOOD MORNING, MAINE

The first place in the United States to be struck by the sun's rays each morning during most of the year is Maine's Cadillac Mountain in Acadia National Park. —*Roads to Adventure*

HOW DO YOU MEASURE UP?

Many of our common measurements originated from the body. The "inch" comes from an Old English word called *ynch* or *unce*, which is the width of a man's thumbnail. The Romans had a measurement called the *palmus,* which was the width of four fingers. And the Egyptian *cubit* referred to the length of a man's arm from the elbow to the tip of his middle finger. —*Parenting*

MATTER OF FAX

The first fax was sent from Lyon to Paris, France—in 1865. *—National Geographic*

RIDE WITH THE TIDE

Because of its higher density, a person floats more easily on saltwater than on freshwater. One of the best places in the world for floating is the Dead Sea.
—Chappies

SILLY STORY

When General Electric was trying to create a rubber substitute during World War II, they invented the gooey stuff we now call Silly Putty. The company sent it to scientists around the world, but they couldn't find anything useful to do with it. *—Reader's Digest*

THICK 'N' CRUSTY

If you removed all the dissolved minerals from the world's oceans and spread them out evenly across the earth's land surface, they would create a salty crust 500 feet thick. —*Popular Science*

PENCIL POINTS

Hexagonal pencils are cheaper to make than round pencils. Nine hexagonal pencils can be made from the same amount of wood as eight round ones. Hexagonal pencils also stay on your desk better!

—*Reader's Digest*

RAINBURGERS

Falling raindrops are shaped more like burger buns than teardrops.

—*React*

BLOWIN' IN THE WIND

Oddly, a 75-mile-per-hour wind has nine times more force than a wind of 25 miles per hour. —*The Weather Channel*

FROZEN BR—

Q: Just how cold can it get in Siberia?

A: Cold enough to freeze human breath so that it drops to the ground and tinkles! —*Reader's Digest*

GOD'S BEAUTIFUL IDEA

Rainbows can be found wherever falling water comes in contact with direct sunlight. That might be a waterfall, a rainstorm, or a garden sprinkler. In the morning look for rainbows in the west, with the sun behind you. During the afternoon look toward the east. At midday you'll find a rainbow only if you are up high looking down on one. —*Reader's Digest*

GRANDER CANYON

The Valles Marineris on Mars makes the United States' Grand Canyon look puny by comparison. The Martian canyon is more than 2,500 miles long, six miles deep, and 12 miles wide. —*Final Frontier*

THE BARROW FACTS

During the summer, Barrow, Alaska, goes 65 days without a sunrise. —*Reader's Digest*

GUILTY AS CHARGED?

A University of Delaware professor studied the remains found in six electric bug zappers (what a job) and found a total of 14,000 dead insects. Only 31 were biting insects, such as mosquitoes. It turns out that mosquitoes are not attracted by the ultraviolet light—instead, they hunt down people by searching for carbon dioxide (from our breath) and for our body heat. By some estimates, more than 70 billion innocent insects get zapped each month! —*E Magazine*

HEY, THAT'S MY NUMBER!

A mathematician has patented a prime number that is 150 digits long. The patent means he owns the number, and no one can use it without his permission! (The long number is valuable because it can be used in secret codes.) —*Scientific American*

YUKKY BUT TRUE

Without saliva, you can't taste food. A dry tongue can't taste the difference between a salty cracker and a spicy pepper. But add a drop of saliva, and all the tastes you love come to life.
—America Online's *Fab Facts*

I CAN'T TASTE A THING!!

CONTINENTAL Q & A:

Q: What continent contains the world's largest body of fresh water and the world's coldest desert?

A: Antarctica. The ice sheet covering the continent contains about 90 percent of the world's ice and 68 percent of the world's fresh water. Then why is Antarctica a desert? Because it gets less than one inch of precipitation a year—making it the *driest* continent on earth!

—Museum of Science and Industry, Tampa, Florida.

DON'T TRY THIS AT HOME

Have you ever wondered how many helium balloons it would take for you to fly? If you're an average 10-year-old, you'd need an estimated 2,450 standard-sized balloons. —*Harper's Index*

COLD HEAT

Even if it's minus 40 degrees outside, an igloo provides such good insulation that you can sit inside without a coat. —*Omni*

MOOOOVE OVER

About one-fourth of the world's landmass is occupied by cattle.
—*The Other Side*

DIGGING IN

The deepest hole ever dug and explored by human beings is just 2.3 miles deep. At that depth, the rock temperature was 131°F.
—*USA Today*

PAPER PUZZLER

Q: How many times can you fold any sheet of paper in half?
A: Just seven times, no matter what the size of the sheet.
—*USA Today*

POWER PACK
The nucleus of a human cell can have more than 100 *million* times more information per unit volume than a computer chip. —*Origins*

RAW FACTS
It takes 10 *tons* of raw ore to produce one ounce of pure platinum.
—*The Platinum Review*

REALLY COOL STATE
The state of Alaska contains about 100,000 glaciers. —*USA Today*

BREAK THE SOUND BARRIER!
To break the sound barrier all you have to do is crack a whip. The sound you're hearing is a miniature sonic boom. —*USA Today*

ARE YOU NUTS?

In the store, cashews don't come in their shells. That's because cashews are relatives of poison ivy, and their shells can create a terrible rash.

—America Online's *Fab Facts*

CORRECT CUTS

There are three reasons cutting a sandwich diagonally is better:

1. A diagonal cut on five-inch-square bread exposes a longer middle surface area (about seven inches) since it is the *hypotenuse* of a triangular wedge.

2. A sandwich cut diagonally tends to lie flat.

3. It's easier to bite into the acute corner of a triangle than the right angle of a rectangular cut.

—*Why Things Are (Volume II): The Big Picture*

BUSINESS IS HURTING

Enjoy honey? Then you'll appreciate knowing that a bee-keeper gets stung 500 times per year on average. —*React*

SAPPY TALK

A maple tree can provide an average of 12 gallons of sap each season. It takes about 40 gallons of sap to make one gallon of pure maple syrup. —*The Secret Life of Food*

FUNGI FIT FOR A KING

Roman emperors liked mushrooms so much that they wouldn't allow ordinary citizens to eat them. They also had their mushrooms cooked in special silver vessels. —*Smithsonian News Service*

THE POD SQUAD ASKS . . .
Q. How many peas will you find in an average pod?
A. Eight. —*Harper's Index*

BOB THE KILLER TOMATO?
Back in the 1500s priests brought tomatoes from South America back to Europe. But many people were afraid to eat the strange new food because they thought tomatoes were poisonous. In fact, it took 300 years for most people to realize that tomatoes are good to eat. —*Ranger Rick*

HOT STUFF
Chili peppers can burn off a runny nose and help prevent heart attacks and strokes. The habanero is the hottest chili pepper ever—up to 50 times as hot as a jalapeño. It can actually raise a welt on the skin. —*Longevity*

DO YOU LIKE PEALEGUMES?

The peanut is not a nut. It's a legume, and grows underground like a potato.
—*React*

MAGNETIC MORNINGS

In the 1970s Kellogg's Frosted Rice cereal contained so much iron that you could pick up kernels with a magnet. —*Bizarro Facts & Radical Earthlings*

HOW SWEET IT IS

Honey never spoils. It remains edible even after thousands of years. —*USA Today*

SOLE FOOD

Imagine having taste buds on your toes! Butterflies don't have to imagine—they actually taste with their feet. —*Bizarro Facts & Radical Earthlings*

NOODLE NEWS

Spinach pasta contains very little spinach—less than a tablespoon per cup of cooked pasta. That doesn't make it much better for you than regular pasta—it only looks and tastes different. —*UC Berkeley Wellness Letter*

LET'S GO UNDERGROUND

When a scientist studied a single rye plant, he discovered 13,800,000 rootlets and root hairs. Placed end to end, this would stretch 387 miles. —*Nature Quest*

COUNTERFEIT BUBBLES

Swiss cheese naturally comes with holes in it, which are caused by expanding gas given off by the bacteria that gives the cheese its flavor. But some cheese makers aren't satisfied with letting nature take its course, so they add the holes using machines! —America Online's *Fab Facts*

THE REFRIGERATOR KNOWS . . .

Eggs stay fresh longer if you store them small end down.
—*Whad'ya Knowledge?*

MARBLE SOUP

One of the tricks some photographers use to make food look more appetizing is to put marbles in soup, which push the vegetables up to the surface. Other tricks include using mashed potatoes for ice cream and white glue for milk. These practices are not allowed in advertisements, but they are used in some cookbooks and food magazines. —*Popular Photographer*

FALSE FRIES

French fries don't come from France. They probably first came from Belgium. —*Did You Ever Wonder . . .*

APPETIZING NAME

John Montagu, a politician who lived in Britain in the 1700s, held the title "Earl of Sandwich." He hated to be interrupted while he played cards, even for meals, so he had his servant bring him a slice of beef between two slices of toast. That's how the "sandwich" got its name. —*Grolier's Encyclopedia*

SPEAKING OF SANDWICHES . . .

If everyone who brought a sack lunch to work or school each day (34 million people) stacked their sandwiches, one on top of the other, the stack would be 11,500 times as tall as the Sears Tower in Chicago. —*USA Today*

OUT OF THIS WORLD
FACTS ABOUT OUTER SPACE

COSMIC HOT SPOT
The largest known volcano is called Olympus Mons, and it's found on Mars. It is 370 miles wide and about three times as high as Mount Everest. —*Omni*

POUNDED BY RAYS
Every second, 4.3 pounds of sunlight hit the earth. —*Harper's Index*

BRING JAM TO VENUS
The planet Venus has two continents whose consistency is similar to peanut butter.
—*Whad'ya Knowledge*

ALL ABOARD FOR THE MOON

Q: How much would a ticket to the moon cost if you paid one cent for every 1,000 miles?

A: $2.40. Based on the same rate, it would cost $930 to fly to the sun, and $260 million to fly to Alpha Centauri, the nearest star.

—*Reader's Digest*

UNIVERSAL PRAISE

When Astronaut Buzz Aldrin visited the moon back in 1969 (along with Neil Armstrong and Michael Collins), he wanted to mark the moment by honoring God. So he observed Communion (the Lord's Supper). —*A Man on the Moon*

HOLD ON TIGHT

On Saturn, winds have blown up to 1,100 miles per hour. —*React*

CELESTIAL SPINNERS

Pulsars are special stars that contain about as much mass as our sun, but are crammed into a space just 10 miles wide. These compact stars "pulse" as they spin at up to several hundred times per *second*. —*Discover*

FREE SPACE TRAVEL

How would you like to travel through space at 1,000 miles an hour? You're already doing it, since you're a passenger on Planet Earth. You're traveling a million miles every six weeks without even leaving your house. —*Omni*

CATCH A FALLING CAR

Each year about a dozen meteors larger than a car enter the earth's atmosphere. —*Harper's Index*

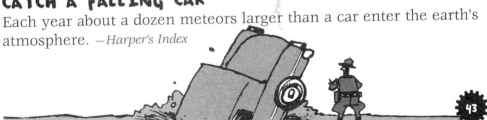

LAVA FLOW ZONES

Some night when the moon is in view, take a look at the dark spots on its surface. Many of these spots are seas of lava. —*Final Frontier*

TWINKLE, TWINKLE LITTLE STARS

Most meteors are no larger than a grain of sand. —*Final Frontier*

ALL-WEATHER THREADS

A typical spacesuit is made up of about 20,000 parts. When an astronaut puts one on and floats around outside the space shuttle, the temperature on the outside of the suit can range between $-250°F$ and $+350°F$.
—*Air & Space*

HEAVY TRUTH

When stars die, they become so dense that a mere spoonful of their matter can weigh several tons. —Wm. Wrigley Jr. Company

HEAVENLY VIEW

Want to get a good view of outer space? A good pair of binoculars will bring all the planets in our solar system into view, with the exception of Pluto. —*Final Frontier*

NOT WITHOUT A CREATOR

"If all the grains of sand on all the beaches of the Earth were possible universes—that is, universes consistent with the laws of physics as we know them—and only one of those grains of sand were a universe that allowed for the existence of intelligent life, then that one grain of sand is the universe we inhabit." —Astronomer Chet Raymo, quoted in *Christianity Today*

SKY-HIGH POSTAGE RATE

What would it cost to mail a letter to space? For every pound the space shuttle launches into orbit, it costs about $12,000. For a one-ounce letter, that would be about $750. —*Final Frontier*

KEEP LOOKING UP

Each year, on average, there is one comet that can be seen with the naked eye. —*Whad'ya Knowledge*

BEWARE OF FALLING AIR

If you paint a baseball, the layer of paint is about as thick, relatively speaking, as the earth's atmosphere. That seems pretty thin. But consider this: If you live at sea level, there is about a *ton* of air molecules floating over your head. —*Omni*

SPACE VINEGAR

Astronomers have discovered a giant cloud of vinegar that is 25,000 light years away from earth.

—*Associated Press*

WHERE'S MY SALAD?!

GOING BY GOD'S BOOK
FACTS ABOUT THE BIBLE AND ITS TIMES

BOO-BOO BIBLE

Those who set the table are especially blessed, according to a Bible printed in 1562. A printer's error in the second edition of the Geneva Bible caused Matthew 5:9 to read: "Blessed are the place-makers." Check out your own Bible to see what it really says.

—*The Complete Book of Bible Trivia*

KEEP 'EM FOREVER

In ancient Egypt, cats were considered sacred. When they died, they were often made into mummies. The British Museum in London contains several hundred Egyptian cat mummies.

—*Fascinating Bible Facts*

"NEW" BIBLE WORDS

When William Tyndale translated the Bible into
English, he "invented" several new words. Can you
guess which of the following words and terms he
introduced?

1. Filthy lucre
2. Scapegoat
3. Peacemaker
4. Longsuffering
5. Beautiful

(Answer: All of them!) —*Christian History*

"GAMBLING" FOR GOD

In the early Christian church there was a group of Christians known as
"the gamblers." They earned this label by caring for people who
had deadly infectious diseases. —*The Daily Bible Study Commentary*

REFORMED REVOLUTIONARY

One of Jesus' disciples may have been a revolutionary before he met Jesus. His name was Simon the Zealot. Although it may just mean he was "zealous," it was also a name of a radical political party that wanted to overthrow the Romans. See Matthew 10:4. —*The Life Application Bible*

STRONG EVIDENCE

There are more ancient copies of the New Testament than any other book of its age. About 24,000 manuscript copies of parts of the New Testament are in existence. The *Iliad*, by Homer, comes in second, with only 643 manuscripts still around today. —*Evidence That Demands a Verdict*

THE WORD FROM CALVARY

When dying on the cross, Jesus referred to His heavenly Father as "Eli" (Matthew 27:46, KJV). This was a form of the Hebrew word *Elohim*, the most commonly used word for God.
—*Fascinating Facts From the Bible*

WHY ARE YOU SHAKING?

Today we shake hands, but in Bible times it was common to greet others by bowing. Depending on whom you were greeting, you could simply nod your head—or bend over completely facedown. *—The Youth Bible*

SCRIPTURE FASHION

The Pharisees wore a box on the forehead and the arm called a phylactery. It contained the following verses: Exodus 13:1-10, 11-16 and Deuteronomy 6:4-9; 11:13-21. *—NIV Study Bible*

THAT'S MY TYPE

Johannes Gutenberg was the inventor of movable type, which he successfully used in 1455 to print Bibles. Gutenberg went bankrupt in the process, however, and died penniless. Today a Gutenberg Bible can be worth $1 million. Of the 200 Bibles Gutenberg printed, some 48 copies exist today.

—Reader's Digest Book of Facts

ALL-AMERICAN BIBLES

No Bibles were printed in the United States until after the Declaration of Independence was signed in 1776. Before that time, all of the Bibles in the American colonies had to be imported from Britain. Why? Only the king's printers were allowed to produce them. —*Christian History*

CORINTH'S CRAZY "CANAL"

The port city of Corinth is located on a small isthmus, or narrow strip of land, that bridges the region of Achaea with the rest of Greece. The Corinth Track was a five-mile rock track that sailors would use as a "canal" to avoid a long and dangerous Mediterranean journey. But unlike a regular canal, the sailors would roll their boats over dry land!

—*The Youth Bible*

DAZZLING CHURCH

The Temple at Jerusalem was being renovated during Jesus' time. King Herod hired 10,000 workers and ordered 1,000 wagons for hauling cream-colored stone. When the job was completed, the Temple shown so brightly in the Mediterranean sun that it was difficult to look at directly. The Temple was destroyed in A.D. 70.
—*The Word in Life Study Bible*

GOING THE EXTRA MILE

When Jesus said, "If someone forces you to go one mile, go with him two miles" (Matthew 5:41), He was referring to a common practice in His day. Roman soldiers often forced civilians to carry their equipment for a mile. —*Fascinating Bible Facts*

THIS BOAT FLOATS

Many other ancient cultures had stories about a great flood. In the Babylonian version, the ark was shaped like a cube and could never float. In contrast, Noah's ark was very seaworthy and stable. Its relative dimensions are similar to that of a modern battleship.

—From a lecture by Bruce Waltke

JARS OF CLAY

In Bible times, people sometimes hid valuable possessions in cheap clay jars, since no one would suspect they contained anything important. That may be what Paul had in mind when he wrote, "But we have this treasure in jars of clay to show that this all-surpassing power is from God and not from us" (2 Corinthians 4:7).

BOOMERANG PROPERTY

According to the laws of ancient Israel, when you sold a piece of property, you automatically got it back after 50 years. This took place during what was called the "jubilee year," and helped ensure that no family remained poor permanently. See Leviticus 25:28.

JESUS DOES IT AGAIN

What are the odds that any person could have coincidentally fulfilled just eight of the Old Testament prophecies of the Messiah? Try one in 100,000,000,000,000,000. —*More Than a Carpenter*

ROAD WARRIORS

To control a vast territory, the emperors of the Roman Empire built a huge network of roads so that their armies could travel quickly from place to place. Altogether, the Roman roads covered a distance of 250,000 miles—enough to circle the earth at the equator 10 times!
—*The Youth Bible*

LAUGH OUT LOUD

Solomon knew what he was talking about when he wrote, "A cheerful heart is good medicine" (Proverbs 17:22). Recently 20 medical students found their white blood cell count (the cells that fight disease) had increased 25 percent after 30 minutes of relaxing and laughing. —*Better Homes and Gardens*

VERY IMPRESSIVE

When Jeremiah delivered prophecies, his assistant, Baruch, wrote them down on scrolls (Jeremiah 36:4). Baruch would seal the scrolls with a special clay imprint that included his name. But on at least one of his seals, he accidentally left a fingerprint, too! The fingerprint of Baruch—owned by a private collector—dates from about 600 B.C., when Jeremiah was predicting the fall of Judah.

—*Christian Reader*

LEADING LADY

At one point in its ancient history, the nation of Israel hadn't won a war for about 175 years. A godly woman named Deborah changed that picture by leading the Israelites to victory over a king named Jabin, whose army included 900 iron-wheeled chariots. For more facts, read Judges 4 and 5.

—*Far Out Facts of the Bible*

LONG-LOST LIBRARY

There are several books and records mentioned in the Bible: the Book of the Wars (Numbers 21:14), the Book of Jashar (Joshua 10:13), the Annals of Solomon (1 Kings 11:41), the book of Gad the seer (1 Chronicles 29:29), the records of Shemaiah the prophet and of Iddo the seer (2 Chronicles 12:15). These lost documents are mainly of a historical nature.

MANUSCRIPT MISTAKE

A 1702 misprint of Psalm 119:161 read, "*Printers* have persecuted me without a cause." The correct word is "princes."

—*The Complete Book of Bible Trivia*

KEEP YOUR SHIRT ON

In Jesus' day Temple guards had to be careful not to sleep on duty. If caught catching Zs, the guard's captain would have the slumberer's clothing stripped off and burned. The disrobed guard was then sent away in disgrace. Revelation 16:15 may refer to this practice. —*The Youth Bible*

WARM-WATER CHURCH

In New Testament Bible times, the city of Laodecia in Asia Minor was rich, but its tap water was disgusting. The water came from hot springs outside of town, but by the time it got to the city it was lukewarm. God said the church in that town was a lot like the water—neither hot nor cold. He said they—and us—needed to make a change! See Revelation 3:14-19. —*Life Application Bible*

BIBLE BARKERS

The Bible mentions dogs two dozen times. There's no reference to domestic cats anywhere in the Bible. —*Fascinating Facts From the Bible*

WHAT'S-HIS-NAME?

The name Caiaphas was a last name. Joseph was the Jewish high priest's first name. He's the one who put Jesus on trial. See Matthew 26:3. —*Fascinating Facts From the Bible*

OLD, BUT STILL WORKS

The oldest complete Bible currently in existence is called the Codex Sinaiticus. It's more than 1,600 years old. A German scholar discovered it on the Sinai Peninsula in 1844. —*The Complete Book of Bible Trivia* and *The Bible in the British Museum*

LET US PRAY

Many consider Psalm 119 as the longest prayer in the Bible, because the entire psalm is directed to God. The longest prayer that is not a psalm is a prayer of praise, confession, and covenant found in Nehemiah 9:5-38.

JESUS' "REAL" NAME

Jesus' friends would have called* Him "Yeshua," the Aramaic word for Jesus. Although Jesus was often called "the Christ," that was not His name at all. Christ is the Greek word for "Messiah," which is a title.
—*Fascinating Bible Facts*

PRECIOUS AND FEW

Before the invention of the printing press, people had to copy the Bible by hand. It was a painfully slow process; it could take 20 scribes an entire year to make just one Bible. —*A History of Christianity*

LIFESAVING CAMPOUT

John 1:14 says, "The Word became flesh and made his dwelling among us." If taken literally, the phrase means the Word "pitched his tent" among us.

NOTES ON POTTERY

Back in Bible times, people wrote notes on broken bits of pottery.
—*Fascinating Bible Facts*

BET I COULD MAKE A <u>BIBLE</u> OUT OF THOSE!

REED 'N' WRITE

The word "bible" (or *biblos* in Greek) refers to the papyrus plant, which was used to make paper. —*Christian History*

LONG AND SHORT

The shortest verse in the Old Testament is 1 Chronicles 1:25: "Eber, Peleg, Reu." The shortest New Testament verse is "Jesus wept" (John 11:35). The longest verse in the Bible is Esther 8:9, containing 90 words (KJV).

SOMEDAY YOU'LL UNDERSTAND

In Jewish culture no one under the age of 30 was allowed to read the first chapter of the book of Ezekiel. The book describes a vision about the glory of God, which Jewish leaders thought was too strange for young readers. —*Fascinating Bible Facts*

THE BODY SHOP
FACTS ABOUT US

EXERCISE OF FREE WILL

Scientists have found that when laboratory animals exercise, it's only good for them if they "work out" voluntarily. Animals that are forced to exercise often lower their immune system, making it easier for them to get sick. (Don't use this excuse with your PE coach. You will probably be reminded that you are not a lab rat.) —*Science News*

FUNNY BUSINESS

An adult laughs an average of 15 times a day. A child, however, laughs an average of 400 times per day. —*Gale Book of Averages*

SNEEZE IN STYLE

The best way to sneeze is into your shoulder, not your hand. Hands can transmit colds more easily. —Tampa *Tribune*

TAKE A DRINK

Some athletes can sweat up to a gallon of water each hour during serious workouts. Even regular folks sweat up to a quart of water during an hour of strenuous exercise. That's why it's so important to drink plenty of water, especially when you're exercising in hot weather. At such times you need to drink water even when you aren't thirsty.

—*UC Berkeley Wellness Letter*

CAN YOU HEAR ME?

Loud concerts can be hazardous to your hearing. Less than 30 minutes of a loud concert (120 decibels) can cause damage to the delicate instruments in your inner ear. If your ears are ringing after the concert, it is a sign of possible damage.

One easy way to protect your ears against any loud, continuous noise is to use earplugs that soften the sound without blocking it completely. —*Zillions*

HOT STUFF

Each day the human body gives off enough heat to melt a 40-pound cake of ice, and then heat the water to the boiling point. —*Ripley's Believe it or Not!*

MONEY GERMS

In the early 1970s, researchers found that 70 percent of the coins and bills in circulation carried potentially harmful bacteria, such as *Streptococcus* and *E. coli.* A more recent study found that only 3 percent of coins and 11 percent of bills are contaminated. One reason for the improvement may be that people wash their hands more often these days.
—*UC Berkeley Wellness Letter*

DON'T BLOW YOUR MIND

Holding in a sneeze can be dangerous—it can cause nosebleeds, damaged nose and eyes, burst eardrums, and even fatal strokes! So, do yourself a favor and let 'er rip—some other direction. —*Outside*

BURNING SODA

To burn off the calories contained in a single can of soda, an average person would have to run for 11 minutes, swim for 18 minutes, or walk for 38 minutes. —*HealthWise*

MITE THIS BE TRUE?

Your eyelashes are home to a tiny, eight-legged critter called *Demodex folliculorum*—better known as a follicle mite. They don't hurt you at all, even though they spend their whole lives on your eyelash. They get all the food they need by puncturing the cells of your eyelash follicles with tiny needles and pumping out cellular fluid. —*Reader's Digest*

FASTER WAY TO THE NBA?

Astronauts tend to grow two inches or more during space flight, since the zero gravity allows the spine to stretch out.
—San Jose *Mercury News*

STRETCHING IT

The skin on an average person measures about 20 square feet, and it accounts for about 20 percent of a person's total body weight.
—*American Health*

LIFE IN THE PRONE ZONE

You burn more calories by sleeping than you do by watching television.
—*Bizarro Facts & Radical Earthlings*

YOU MAKE ME SICK

Anger can make you more likely to catch a cold. If cancer or heart disease runs in your family, anger may also make you more vulnerable to these diseases. —*HealthWise*

GONE IN A BLINK OF AN EYE

If you added up all the times you'll blink in a lifetime (about six times a minute or more), it will total nearly a year. —*Tidbits*

HAIRY TALE

The hair follicles on your head stay alive for up to six years. That gives them the opportunity to grow to lengths of up to three feet—even longer for some people.
—America Online's *Fab Facts*

HIGH GUYS

Back in 1850 American men were the tallest humans. They averaged five feet six inches—but now they average five feet eight inches. American men are no longer the tallest, however. The average Dutchman stands five feet ten inches tall—up six inches from 1850. (Women typically measure about five inches less than men do.) —*Discover*

CATFISH WITH TASTE

Human beings have about 9,000 taste buds. Birds, on the other hand, have only about 500. But a rabbit is the proud owner of 17,000 taste buds, while a cow has about 35,000. The taste-bud champ, however, is the catfish, which has 100,000. —*Nature Quest*

HAIR-RAISING FACT

The average human body produces about seven miles of hair each year and about 350 miles of hair in a lifetime. *—Omni*

HEAD START

All the neurons in your brain were formed by the time you were born. That means they developed at the rate of 150 *per second* during nine months of pregnancy. *—Addiction and Grace*

WATER WORKS

The human body is about 73 percent water. *—React*

FUNNY WAY TO EXERCISE

If you laugh 100 times a day, it's about the same amount of exercise as spending 10 minutes on a rowing machine, according to Dr. William Fry of Stanford University. *—Omni*

IS THAT A FACT?

If you learned one new fact every second, day and night, your brain has room to keep learning for 3 million years. Your brain can hold about 94,608,000,000,000 facts! —*Moody Bible Institute*

LIFESAVING SNAKES

Some snake poisons contain a substance that prevents blood from clotting. This same substance might be used to prevent blood clots that can trigger heart attacks in human beings. Scientists are studying the venom of many poisonous snakes to see if they can discover a medicine that would save thousands of lives each year. —*National Geographic*

I'M STUFFED!

FACTS

CANDY CURE

Licorice has been used in ancient cultures as a cold medicine, wound healer, and asthma treatment. Modern scientists believe licorice could be good for sore throats and possibly boost your immune system. (Most candy licorice is artificial, not the "good" stuff! Genuine licorice comes from cooking the root of a plant called *Glycryrrhiza glabra*.) —*UC Berkeley Wellness Letter*

NEED MORE Z'S?

According to the National Sleep Foundation, young people ages 10-14 need nine to 10 hours of sleep every night. —*Healthy Bites*

LOOSEN UP

Many people think that wearing hats can cause permanent hair loss. They're wrong. But be careful with tight ponytails and braids. Years of wearing tightly braided hair can cause root damage.

—*American Health*

ROMAN TOOTHPICKS

Toothpicks made from vulture quills give you bad breath, according to Pliny the Younger (A.D. 61-113). He suggested using a quill from a porcupine instead, since it "makes the teeth firm." —*Oral-B*

SUPER DROOLER

Your body produces up to 1.4 quarts of saliva each day. —*The Walking Magazine*

I'M DOWN A QUART.

SICK FACT

The bacteria-infested water droplets from a sneeze can float in the air for 40 minutes. —*Omni*

BABIES WITH NERVE

A newborn baby has more nerve cells in his or her brain than an adult. —Tampa *Tribune*

IT'S ALL IN YOUR HEAD

Every neuron (brain cell) in your head has about 20,000 synapses (or connections to other cells). That means there are about 500 trillion synapses in your brain. If you had a computer to count synapses at the rate of a thousand a second, it would take up to *15,000 years* to count them all.
—Addiction and Grace

KILLER COFFEE

In sixteenth-century Turkey, drinking a hot cup of coffee was punishable by death. *—It's a Fact*

THE HOLE TRUTH

Each day about 1 million people in the United States visit a dentist. And each day about 500,000 cavities are filled. *—HealthWise*

THINK FAST!

Most people speak at a rate of about 150 to 200 words a minute. But most of us think at a rate of 1,300 words a minute. *—Worry-free Living*

TOO COLD TO CATCH COLD

In spite of its chilly temperature, you won't catch a cold at the North Pole in winter. Cold and flu bugs apparently like climates that are a little less frosty.
—*USA Today*

WIRY HAIR

A single strand of human hair is stronger than a copper wire of the same thickness. —*Omni*

PING PONG PAIN

Table tennis players are injured more often than skydivers or bungee jumpers. —New York *Times Magazine*

PRUNE FINGERS

Why do your fingers wrinkle up like prunes when they've been soaking for a long time? It's because the outer layer of skin (called the *stratum corneum*) absorbs water and expands. Since there's nowhere for it to expand to, it just wrinkles. —*Chicago Reader*

WATER WONDERLAND

FACTS ABOUT FISH AND OTHER SEA LIFE

FREQUENT FLOATERS

Gray whales migrate 12,000 miles each year—from Alaska to Baja California. —*National Geographic World*

NOSEY SHARKS

A great white shark finds its prey by smell. These sharks often stick their noses out of the water to sniff the air for the scent of prey.
—*Wildlife Explorer*

SEA, I'M WALKING!

The batfish walks along the ocean floor, using its lower fins as feet.
—*Ripley's Believe It or Not*

FISH OUT OF WATER

The small silver fish called grunions actually lay their eggs on land. At high tide during spring and summer they throw themselves up on the beaches of California, lay their eggs, then flip their way back into the water. The eggs will hatch about two weeks later during high tide.

—*Audubon*

HARD OF HEARING

Fishes' ears are made of stone. The ear stone, called an otolith, is made of calcium carbonate. It picks up vibrations in the water around the fish. —*Boy's Life*

SWEET DREAMS

Parrotfish have a clever way of protecting themselves from their enemies. When a parrotfish wants to sleep, it secretes a jellylike bubble around itself. Enemies can't get to the parrot fish through this bubble. However, the bubble takes 30 minutes to make and to break.

—*The Usborne Book of Ocean Facts*

GOING MY WAY?

Hitchhiking is not a good way to travel—unless you're a remora fish. These ocean fish have a sort of suction cup on the top of their heads, which they use to catch a ride aboard sea turtles.
—*Ranger Rick*

VERTICAL JUMPERS

A penguin can leap up to seven feet out of the water. —*USA Today*

SON OF SIAM

Not all Siamese fighting fish are quick to pick a fight. Some of the males watch fights from a distance to see which fish win most often. That way they can avoid starting a dangerous fight with a stronger fish. —*Science News*

SEA FLEAS

The tiny sea flea, about the size of a pinhead, is a great traveler. It must swim to the sea surface at night to find food. When dawn arrives, it returns to the deep sea for safety. This journey is 1,312 feet deep, and it travels this distance each day. Considering the size and distance, the flea's daily trip is the same as a human swimming 400 miles a day. —*The Usborne Book of Ocean Facts*

HEY, BIG BIVALVE

The largest bivalve shell (a shell with two halves) is the giant clam, which can grow more than four feet long and weigh 500 pounds. —*Ranger Rick*

SHOOTOUT!

The Mexican dancer sea slug eats sea anemones that have stinging cells. These stinging cells then travel through the sea slug's body and come to rest just under the skin. If an enemy touches the slug, the stinging cells shoot out into them, chasing the enemy away. —*The Usborne Book of Ocean Facts*

DOLPHIN NOSE GEAR

When bottlenose dolphins hunt for food on the sandy sea bottom near Western Australia, they risk getting stung in the face by stingrays and other critters. So the dolphins jam a sea sponge on their beaks to protect themselves during the hunt. —*National Geographic*

SUPER SNOOPERS

The sense of smell is extremely important to sharks, since that's how they hunt. In fact, nearly two thirds of their brain is devoted to processing scent information.
—*Wildlife Fact File*

OH, THAT'S DEEP

Penguins dive deeper into the ocean in search of food than any other nonmarine animal. Penguins have been recorded at depths of 785 feet. —*Ripley's Believe It or Not!*

DON'T MESS WITH STONY

The stonefish enjoys double protection against its enemies. When the stonefish is lying on the sea floor, it looks like a weed-covered rock. If an enemy should discover the fish and decide to attack, the stonefish depends on 13 very sharp, poisonous spines sticking out of its back.
—*The Usborne Book of Ocean Facts*

HUMAN ATTACK!

For every human being killed by a shark, *10 million* sharks are killed by human beings. —*Audubon*

I CAN FLY!

I'M OUTTA HERE

Flying fish can glide for distances of up to 60 feet and at speeds of up to 40 miles per hour. After getting up to speed, the fish leap out of the water and glide—using their large pectoral fins as wings. —*Outside*

HANG IN THERE

The janthina snail lives on the surface of the sea. In order to stay afloat, the snail blows bubbles. It blows one each minute and joins them all together to form a raft. The snail then hangs upside down from the bubble raft and feeds from this position.

—*Usborne Book of Ocean Facts*

WALK THIS WAY

Crabs can walk backward and forward, but they always run sideways when they're in a hurry. Seems they're less likely to trip that way. The fastest crab is the ghost crab, which can reach speeds of up to five miles per hour on dry land.

—*Virginia Marine Science Museum*

SEA MONSTER LIVES!

The giant squid can grow to lengths of 60 feet and weigh more than a ton. They have eyes the size of hubcaps. But as big as they are, biologists have never seen a giant squid in the wild. Almost everything we know about giant squids comes from dead specimens that have washed up onshore. —*USA Today*

WHO YOU CALLIN' SHRIMP?

Brine shrimp may be small, but they're almost impossible to kill. You can freeze them, dry them out completely, or even expose them to toxic chemicals without harming them. Even after brine shrimp eggs have been dried up for years, they still hatch. All they need is saltwater. —*National Geographic World*

GOD'S GREAT BIG GARDEN
FACTS ABOUT PLANTS AND OTHER GROWING THINGS

KING OF THE CACTI

The saguaro cactus can live up to 175 years, grow up to 50 feet high, and weigh six tons. What's its secret to survival? It is 95 percent water. The cactus sometimes looks like a stick person because of its outstretched arms. But the prickly plant doesn't start its arms until it's 50 years old.

—*National Geographic Traveler and Sierra*

LIFE IN THE FOREST

About two thirds of all species of life on earth live in rain forests.

—Tampa's Museum of Science and Industry

WORLD-CLASS SEED

A palm tree in the Seychelles Islands produces a seed that grows up to 20 inches long—making it the biggest known seed in the world. —*React*

LONG-LASTING LICHENS

Lichens are actually two cooperating plants, colorful fungi that team up with algae. They coat rocks all over the world and thrive in some of the harshest conditions on earth. They may live as long as 1,000 years. —*Audubon*

WOOD YOU BELIEVE . . .

Forests in the eastern United States are growing back. They now cover about the same amount of land as they did before the American Revolution. —*Environment*

LILY IS GROWING FAST

The world's fastest-growing plant is the giant water lily, which grows almost a foot each day. —*3-2-1 Contact*

FEATHERED FRIENDS
FACTS ABOUT BIRDS

LOOK ME IN THE EARS
A bird named the woodcock has ears located between its eyes and bill rather than on the sides of its head. —*Ranger Rick*

BIRD'S-EYE VIEW
If you had eyes as powerful as a peregrine falcon, you could read a newspaper from 100 yards away. —*Southern Living*

SCAREDY-BIRD
The ostrich doesn't hide its head in the sand when danger comes. Instead, it usually runs. The ostrich is the world's largest bird, and it can cover 25 feet in a single stride, reaching speeds of up to 60 miles per hour. —*Fascinating Facts*

WHOOO'S HOME?

The elf owl of the southwestern United States makes its home inside a giant cactus. —*Ripley's Believe It or Not!*

I WANNA GO HOME

A pigeon can find its way home from 1,500 miles away. —*Northwest Airlines*

BRING BACK MY HAIR!

The tufted titmouse (a bird that lives in the eastern U.S.) likes to use hair for building its nests. And it will go to great lengths to get it. The titmouse has been known to pull hairs from live opossums, woodchucks, squirrels, and even people.

—*Falcon*

STEADY NOW

A hummingbird's heart can beat up to 1,200 times a minute. Compare that to your own heart: If you ran as fast as you could, the most your heart would beat is about 200 times a minute. —*Ranger Rick*

INSIDE INFORMATION

You'd think woodpeckers would have a hard time hearing with all that racket they make—but they actually use their powerful hearing to locate insects that are hidden inside trees. —*React*

SHOUT IT OUT

Cranes can fly at altitudes of 30,000 feet, which is higher than Mount Everest. Because of their extra-long windpipe, their voice can be heard two miles away.

—*Ripley's Believe It or Not* and the Ocala *Star-Banner*

CUCKOO FAMILY VALUES

Instead of building a nest of her own, a female cuckoo bird "borrows" the nest of another bird. When the other bird flies away for a moment, the cuckoo bird lands, pushes out an egg from the other bird, and lays her own egg in its place. The cuckoo then leaves and lets the other bird raise her chick. —*National Geographic World*

THAT'S EGGSTRA-ORDINARY!

The ostrich egg yolk is the largest single cell found in nature.
—Museum of Science and Industry (Tampa, Florida)

DID YOU SEA THAT?

The blue-footed booby is a Central American bird that earned its name because of its clumsiness on land. But the bird is an ace hunter, diving from heights of 80 feet to pluck out fish swimming near the surface of the water, sometimes in midair. —*Wildlife Fact File*

SCARY DECORATION

Australia's riflebird always decorates its nest with a snakeskin in order to frighten away predators. —*Ripley's Believe it or Not!*

SKY HIGH

The highest bird flight on record is that of a Ruppell's vulture, which was once recorded flying at 12,609 meters (41,370 feet) above Africa's Ivory Coast. How was the bird found at this altitude? The poor creature flew into an airplane. —*Outside*

FOLLOW THE LEADER

People who study geese still don't know exactly why the birds fly in V-shaped formations. Two possible reasons: it's the easiest way to keep an eye on each other, or perhaps they save energy by flying in the updraft caused by the flight path of another goose. —*Outside*

PARROT'S NIGHT OUT

When one man's yellow-naped Amazon parrot accidentally flew away, the bird was returned to him the very next day. The bird had been in the same room as the owner's answering machine and had memorized the message and phone number. —*Reader's Digest*

STURDY BIRDIE HOME

Many birds build new nests every year, but not the bald eagle. The bald eagle mates for life and builds only one nest, to which it adds every year. Some eagles' nests can weigh as much as a ton! —*Incredible Facts*

OVER THE SPEED LIMIT

Mourning doves fly at an average speed of 70 miles per hour.
   A mallard, however, cruises at 55 miles per hour.
      —*Ducks Unlimited*

DOWN TO EARTH
FACTS ABOUT THE PLANET WE CALL HOME

ALL SHOOK UP
Every day more than 9,000 earthquakes of magnitude 4.9 or less take place somewhere in the world. *—USA Today*

COSMIC PUNCHING BAG
Up to 150 tons of meteorite fragments slam into the earth every year. *—Omni*

WAY-DOWN WATER
Crater Lake in Oregon is the deepest lake in the United States. It was formed by a gigantic volcanic eruption, and it is almost 2,000 feet deep. *—Newsweek*

BIG MISTAKE

One of California's largest lakes was created by accident. The Salton Sea didn't exist until 1905, when engineers attempted to divert water from the Colorado River to California's Imperial Valley. The river flooded and burst through a dike, creating the massive Salton Sea, which is 225 feet below sea level. —*Audubon*

AS COLD AS IT GETS

On July 21, 1983, scientists at Vostok Station, Antarctica, recorded the lowest temperature ever: 128.6 degrees below zero.
—Tampa *Tribune*

CORNY POLLUTION SOLUTION

Growing one acre of corn removes 200,000 pounds of carbon dioxide from the atmosphere each year. —Paul Harvey

EARTH'S INNER SPINNER

The earth's core—a ball of solid iron 1,500 miles wide—actually spins faster than the rest of the planet. In fact, it outpaces the earth's surface by one turn every 400 years! —*Discover*

DRY FACT

If you think Death Valley sounds dry, maybe you should visit the Atacama Desert in Chile. According to the local weather report, there's been less than an inch of rain in the past century.

—*Final Frontier*

TWISTER TWIVIA

About 900 tornadoes form every year in the United States. Most tornadoes last only a few minutes, but in 1917 a single tornado lasted nearly 8 hours and traveled more than 250 miles across Illinois and Indiana. —*Essentials of Physical Geography Today*

WORLD'S BIGGEST HOT SPOT

The Sahara in North Africa is about the size of the United States. It grows as much as 4 kilometers each year, and the temperature there once reached 136°F. —*Kids for Saving Earth*

SHARING, CARING FORESTS

Scientists have learned that the trees in a forest share their food. Here's how it works: Some trees get more than enough nutrients, while others might go hungry. But underground, a vast network of roots and fungi makes sure the food is evenly distributed. —*Discover*

BITING COLD

Q: Just how cold can it get in Antarctica?
A: Cold enough to crack the enamel off your teeth. —*Outside*

ATTACKED BY ELECTRONS!

Earth periodically gets bombarded with what scientists call "killer electrons," that can actually disable satellites and power grids. Astronomers have known that the sun was responsible, but now it turns out that Jupiter also sometimes blasts Earth with similar super-powered electrons. This new information will help scientists make better predictions of the "weather" in outer space. —*USA Today*

YOU CLIMBED WHAT HILL?

The longest name for a place in the world is a hill in New Zealand called Taumatawhakatangihangakoauotamateaturipukakapikimaunga-horonukupokaiwhenuakitanataha. Say it three times fast. —*React*

CHIPS OFF THE OLD BLOCK

If all the diamonds ever found were put together in a single cube, it would measure only about 10 feet on each side. —*USA Today*

TUNES FROM DUNES

Some sand dunes actually "sing." This strange phenomenon takes place all over the world. Scientists think they know why certain sand dunes hum when the wind blows over them. Singing sand dunes contain more silica than ordinary sand. When silica gets damp, it creates a gel that causes the sand to stick together. Then when the wind comes, the whole dune vibrates in unison. *—Discover*

BLUE PLANET WEIGHS IN

Planet Earth weighs 6.6 quadrillion tons. *—USA Today*

LONG, HOT SUMMER

The longest days of the year are near June 21, the summer solstice, when the sun reaches its highest point in the Northern Hemisphere. But the *hottest* days in the year usually come a month later, when the heat of longer days has had time to accumulate. *—USA Today*

NEW FAITHFUL
Out in the middle of Nevada's Hualapai Flat, there's a spectacular geyser that boils up steaming hot water 24 hours a day. But this isn't any ordinary geyser—it was created by accident in 1916 when ranchers drilling a well tapped a vein of water that can be as hot as 220°F. —*Natural History*

QUICK AS A FLASH!
In the time it takes to read this sentence, lightning has flashed more than 500 times on this planet. —*OMNI*

DEEP SECRETS
The deepest spot in the world—the Mariana Trench (a long depression in the floor of the Pacific Ocean)—is so deep that it could hide Mount Everest! The Mariana Trench is 36,198 feet deep, 45 miles wide, and more than 1,700 miles long. —*Reader's Digest*

THE SKY IS FALLING

Most hailstones are pretty small, but throughout history people have reported giant chunks of ice falling from the sky. Hailstones from 20 feet in diameter to the size of elephants have been reported (but not con-

firmed). The largest *confirmed* hailstone fell in Coffeyville, Kansas, on September 3, 1970. Its circumference was 17.2 inches, and it weighed in at a pound and a half. —*Audubon Society Field Guide to North American Weather*

HAWAIIAN ACTIVITY

The two major Hawaiian volcanoes, Mauna Loa and Kilauea, are the most active volcanoes in the world. They've erupted more than 100 times in the past two centuries. —*Audubon*

VERY HIGH WINDS

The strongest wind ever measured occurred on April 12, 1934, on New Hampshire's Mount Washington. The wind was clocked at 231 miles per hour. —*USA Today*